SKY PIONEER

SKY PIONEER

A Photobiography of Amelia Earhart

By Corinne Szabo

NATIONAL
GEOGRAPHIC
SOCIETY

Washington, D.C.

For Nancy, Peter, and Dan – C.S.

TITLE PAGE: With arms swinging, Amelia strides confidently in front of her Lockheed Electra.
OPPOSITE PAGE: Her pilot's license gives her birthday as July 24, 1898, but her birth certificate,
family bible, and other sources record the year as 1897.

PUBLISHED BY THE
NATIONAL GEOGRAPHIC SOCIETY
1145 17TH ST., NW, WASHINGTON, D.C. 20036

REG MURPHY, *President and Chief Executive Officer.*
GILBERT M. GROSVENOR, *Chairman of the Board.*
NINA D. HOFFMAN, *Senior Vice President.*
WILLIAM R. GRAY, *Vice President and Director of the Book Division.*
Staff for this book: BARBARA LALICKI, *Director of Children's Publishing.*
SUEZ KEHL, *Art Director.* GRETA ARNOLD, *Illustrations Editor.*
BARBARA BROWNELL, *Senior Editor.* MARK CARALUZZI, *Marketing Manager.*
CORINNE SZABO, *Picture Researcher and Original Layout Designer.*
CARL MEHLER, *Map Editor and Designer.* TRACEY M. WOOD, *Map Researcher.*
MICHELLE H. PICARD AND JOHN S. BALLAY, *Map Production.*
LEWIS R. BASSFORD, *Production Project Manager.*
MEREDITH WILCOX, *Illustrations Assistant.* DALE HERRING, *Editorial Assistant.*
VINCENT P. RYAN, *Manufacturing and Quality Manager.*
RICK DAVIS, *Indexer.*

Library of Congress Cataloging-in-Publication Data
Szabo, Corinne
Sky pioneer : a photobiography of Amelia Earhart / by Corinne Szabo
p. cm.
Includes index.
Summary: A biography, with numerous photographs and quotes from Earhart herself,
tracing this determined woman's life and interest in flying.
ISBN 0-7922-3737-4
1. Earhart, Amelia, 1897-1937-Juvenile literature. 2. Earhart,
Amelia, 1897-1937-Portraits-Juvenile literature. 3. Air pilots-
United States-Biography-Juvenile literature. [1. Earhart,
Amelia, 1897-1937. 2. Air pilots. 3. Women-Biography.] I. Title.
TL540.E3S97 1997
629.13'092--dc20 [B] 96-32763

To want in one's head to do a thing,

for its own sake; to enjoy doing it;

to concentrate all of one's energies upon it—

that is not only

the surest guarantee of its success.

It is also being true to oneself."

Amelia's Electra flies above San Francisco Bay and just beneath the clouds for a trial flight early in 1937.

FOREWORD

AMELIA EARHART is one of America's most famous women. As a pilot, she set many records for altitude, speed, and distance; but it is what she did with her life that is important. It is her grace in the face of adversity, and her ironclad determination to overcome whatever stood in her way—whether it was a family life that was rough at times, or low expectations of women. She demonstrated that everyone has the ability to do more, and to be more.

Amelia worked hard to achieve her goals. She and other women pilots faced the same dangers, took the same risks, and set the same records as all pilots of that early era. But women pilots were considered "different," not competent, and so were not taken seriously. Women had to prove their ability constantly. Pioneers like Amelia Earhart made it possible for them to believe in themselves and to follow their dreams.

Amelia said herself in many different ways that she was not afraid to fail. This is a characteristic always present in people who achieve greatness. Amelia wrote, "Women must try to do things as men have tried. When they fail, their failure must be but a challenge to others."

Amelia's challenge has inspired me as a pilot, and as a person. Like Amelia, I worked hard for many years to pay for flying lessons, gas, and airplanes. Amelia taught me that I could do whatever I wanted with my life. She refused to accept boundaries set by society or those around her. She never gave up.

To have a dream and achieve a goal, you must never give up. You must use every day to take a step, even a small step, toward that goal. Always remember Amelia's message. You too can dream "big dreams," and in spite of the challenges you encounter in your life, you can accomplish your heart's desires.

If Amelia had not been lost, it is likely that history would have focused only on her dedication, skill, courage, and daring. This is the Amelia Earhart we should remember and celebrate.

LINDA FINCH
World Flight 1997 Pilot, San Antonio, Texas

ABOVE: Amelia, dressed up in a lacy party dress at age six, loved growing up
in her grandparents' 11-room house (at right). She was always an avid reader and spent
many hours browsing the crowded shelves in Grandfather Otis's large library.

It ALL BEGAN HIGH ON A BLUFF overlooking the Missouri River in her grandparents' large and wonderful house in Atchison, Kansas. This is where Amelia Earhart was born on July 24, 1897.

Her father, Edwin Earhart, worked for the railroads in their claims department. His job required a lot of travel and his wife, Amy, often accompanied him, leaving Amelia and her younger sister, Muriel, in the care of their grandparents during the school year.

At the turn of the century it was considered improper for girls to participate in "boys' activities." Happily, the Earharts did not hold this view. They encouraged their daughters to be inventive, independent, and imaginative.

Amelia and Muriel, on a porch of their grand-parents' home in Atchison, in 1902.

9

Amelia's parents, Amy and Edwin Earhart, married on October 16, 1895. Amy's father, Judge Otis, would not permit the marriage to take place until he was assured of Edwin's ability to support Amy. This took five years. After he agreed to the match, the judge presented the young couple with their own home, fully furnished, just 22 miles away in Kansas City.

Amelia later said that her childhood was filled with "good times." Her pleasant memories were of games, school (she loved to read), mud-ball fights, and picnics. She enjoyed fishing and playing football with her father and collecting bugs and insects with her mother. In summer, she played along the bluffs and explored nearby sandstone caves with Muriel and neighborhood friends. In winter, she favored what grown-ups called "the tomboy method of sledding"—belly flopping.

Occasionally Edwin would pack up the family and take them on a long trip. Amelia visited cities in Iowa and Minnesota, going as far west as California, sometimes in a private railroad car.

The adventure of travel fascinated her.

With Muriel and their cousins, she would take perilous, make-believe journeys in an old abandoned carriage in her grandparents' barn. "Together," Amelia said, "we traveled far and wide through hair-raising adventures without ever leaving the barn." She loved looking at maps and would make the carriage "horses" dash toward the faraway places they pictured.

Amelia called these early experiences "threads" that led her to aviation.

*T*he maps
of far places
that fell into
our clutches
supplemented the
hair-raising
experiences of the
decrepit carriage....
The map of Africa
was a favorite."

Their forward-looking
mother had gym suits with
bloomer bottoms made
so that Amelia, on stilts,
and Muriel, on the swing,
would be comfortable
playing outdoors.

This family picture was taken in Atchison around 1907. From left: Amelia's sister, Muriel; her uncle, Carl Otis; her grandmother, Amelia Harres Otis; Amelia; her aunt, Mrs. Carl Otis; and her parents, Amy Otis Earhart and Edwin Earhart.

Edwin Earhart received a promotion in 1905 that took him and Amy to Des Moines, Iowa, where they bought a house. Their two daughters stayed in Atchison to attend school. In the summer of 1908, the girls joined their parents in Des Moines.

That same year, to celebrate Amelia's 11th birthday, her father took the family to the Iowa State Fair.

When Amelia attended the Iowa State Fair in 1908, it probably looked much the same as it does in this photo taken around 1910. Her favorite purchase was "an absurd hat made of an inverted peach basket."

At the fair Amelia saw on display her first airplane, one made of wood and very rusty metal. She was not at all impressed, probably preferring the Ferris wheel and pony rides.

Throughout her teens, Amelia's family moved a lot. Her father had developed a serious drinking problem, and he was forced to find a position with another railroad company. Over the years, his jobs were often in jeopardy. The Earharts lived in Kansas City, Des Moines, St. Paul, and Chicago.

Can you imagine what it would be like to attend six high schools before graduating? Breaking off friendships and pulling up roots?

Looking back at her teenage years, Amelia saw the positive side. Perhaps she had missed some things by not staying in one place for a long time, but she'd benefited by learning to adapt to new surroundings quickly.

Later in life, when she would meet a stranger who claimed to be from her hometown, her reply was, "Which one?"

Airplanes were a curiosity in 1908 when Amelia saw her first plane. Just five years earlier the Wright Brothers made the world's first powered flight, remaining in the air for 12 seconds. Still a novelty at the 1911 Iowa State Fair, the flight of a Burgess-Wright plane was a grandstand event.

As a volunteer during World War I, Amelia felt very pleased by her gray-and-white nurse's aide uniform. But she thought wearing bright colors would be more cheerful for the patients: "It's a pet theory of mine that color in a drab world can go a long way in stimulating morale."

Amelia went on to college preparatory school, the Ogontz School near Philadelphia. During her last year she decided to spend her winter vacation visiting Muriel, who was attending college in Toronto, Canada.

It was December 1917. America had only recently started to fight in World War I, but the war had been going on in Europe since 1914. Walking the streets of Toronto, Amelia was shocked to see so many wounded English and Canadian soldiers. She was so saddened by their condition that she decided to stay awhile and find a way to help. After completing a Red Cross course, she worked as a nurse's aide at Spadina Military Hospital and became friendly with some of the wounded pilots.

On her day off, she would ride horses with her sister or visit a nearby airfield to watch her former patients practice flying. She stayed on at the hospital until shortly after the war ended on November 11, 1918.

RIGHT: While Amelia worked in Toronto with the returning wounded, these American soldiers were treated in a military hospital in France.

BELOW: The Red Cross helped many soldiers in Europe.

I believe it was in the winter of 1918 that I became interested in airplanes. Though I had seen one or two at county fairs before, I now saw many of them, as the officers were trained at the various fields around the city....I hung around in spare time and absorbed all I could....I remember well that when the snow blown back by the propellers stung my face, I felt a first urge to fly."

17

As soon as we left the ground, I knew I myself had to fly....'I think I'd like to learn to fly,' I told the family casually that evening, knowing full well I'd die if I didn't. 'Not a bad idea,' said my father just as casually. 'When do you start?'"

Working in the hospital had a strong effect on Amelia. When she returned to the United States, she enrolled at Columbia University as a premedical student. After her first year, her parents, who were living in Los Angeles, begged her to come visit. It was the summer of 1920.

Air shows were popular weekend entertainment. Often dragging her father along, Amelia went to all the nearby air circuses. Caught up in the excitement, she took her first ride in an airplane and found it thrilling.

She struggled to earn money for flying lessons and worked for a while as a clerk at the telephone company. Eventually, with her mother's help, she bought her own plane, a Kinner Airster. The final payment was made on July 24, 1922, her 25th birthday.

During the four years she spent in California, Amelia Earhart put in many hours of flying. In May of 1923 she earned her pilot's license from the Fédération Aéronautique Internationale.

Amelia took her first flying lessons from Neta Snook (at left) in 1921. They became great friends and often double-dated. Amelia painted her first plane, a Kinner Airster, bright yellow—and called it *Canary*.

OPPOSITE: This photo appears on Amelia's pilot's license.

By the spring of 1924, her parents' marriage, which had been troubled on and off for many years, was finally coming to an end.

Once Amelia realized that she would be unable to help save it, she was anxious to return to the East Coast. She sold her plane, bought a yellow convertible sports car, and drove her mother cross-country to join Muriel, who was then living in Boston.

After another stint at Columbia, she decided that medical school was not for her. When she returned to Boston in 1925, Amelia found a job as a social worker at Denison House, a Boston community center. She taught English to Syrian, Chinese, Italian, and Irish immigrants, and helped them to become settled in their new country.

Amelia believed that education was the surest way to help them improve their lives. She often visited immigrant families in their homes, sometimes staying for a meal. She was adored by the children, and throughout her life she never forgot them.

Amelia nicknamed her yellow Kissel sports car "The Yellow Peril." It was a favorite with the children at Denison House, who often climbed on top for a ride around the block.

LEFT: Amelia met Sam Chapman, a tall, handsome engineer, while he was a boarder in her parents' Los Angeles home. They enjoyed each other's company and became close friends. Hoping to marry Amelia, Sam followed her when she went back east to Boston. However, Amelia wanted to pursue her career, and Sam did not want a working wife. She turned down his proposal, but they remained good friends. He was one of the few to watch Amelia take off from Boston Harbor in 1928.

Amelia continued to fly in her spare time. She joined the local chapter of the National Aeronautics Association (NAA), attended their lectures, and became known to others in the organization. One April afternoon in 1928, while in the midst of dealing with children's problems at Denison House, she reluctantly answered the phone. It was to be a major turning point.

The man on the line said that she'd been recommended by a member of the NAA as a person who might be interested in doing something for aviation—even though it could be hazardous. Intrigued, she set up a meeting and heard about a daring plan.

Amy Phipps Guest, an American heiress who was married to an Englishman, wanted to sponsor a flight that would carry the first woman passenger across the Atlantic to England. As she could not do it herself, she was looking for a well-educated American woman with a pleasing appearance and manner—who was also a pilot—to make the trip.

George Palmer Putnam, a prominent publisher, led the search. He met with Amelia at his New York office. Shortly afterward, she was told she'd been selected.

Thrilled to have the opportunity, and in spite of the dangers, Amelia accepted. She was thirty-one years old.

BOTTOM LEFT: Charles Lindbergh became a hero and a celebrity after he made the first solo flight across the Atlantic in 1927. Amelia, having impressed her interviewers with her strong qualifications and her "extraordinary resemblance" to Lindbergh, was chosen to make a record-breaking transatlantic journey that would give her similar fame.

RIGHT: Amelia was photographed a few days before the flight dressed in full pilot's regalia—helmet, leather jacket, riding breeches, and leather boots.

In a telegram to her mother before the flight, Amelia wrote:

*D*on't worry.
No matter what happens
it will have been worth
the trying."

In those days, there were very few women who would even consider such an offer. Newspapers screamed headlines such as "Boston Social Worker To Fly Atlantic" and "Girl Pilot Dares the Atlantic."

After much preparation and many delays, pilot Wilmer Stultz took his place at the controls and flight mechanic Lou Gordon climbed into the copilot's seat. Amelia positioned herself just behind the cockpit between two gasoline tanks, where she recorded impressions in her log book.

The plane, the *Friendship*, took off from Trepassey, Newfoundland, on June 17, 1928. It landed 20 hours and 40 minutes later in Burry Port, Wales.

24

Flying much of the way across the Atlantic in heavy fog, the *Friendship*, a trimotor Fokker specially fitted with pontoons for a water landing, rests in the harbor at Burry Port, Wales. More than 2,000 townspeople gathered at the shore for a look at the woman aviator before the plane took off for Southampton, England.

TOP: Amelia poked her head from the fuselage door after arriving at Southampton from Burry Port. Amy Guest, the sponsor of the flight, owned the plane. She'd named it *Friendship* as a symbol of goodwill between England and America.

RIGHT: On the official launch that brought them ashore at Southampton, Amelia had her first meeting with Amy Guest (seated left).

FAR RIGHT: Pilot Wilmer Stultz (at left), Amelia, and mechanic Lou Gordon wave to the welcoming crowds in New York City after their triumphant return.

26

Amelia's daring and courage were acclaimed all over the world. The banner headline across the New York *World*'s front page exclaimed, "First Woman Flies Atlantic."

Amelia did not feel that her role as a passenger should make her a heroine. She hoped someday to pilot a plane across the ocean— "to prove that I deserved at least a small fraction of the nice things said about me."

Flying now became the center of Amelia's life. She left her job at Denison House, and at George Putnam's urging, devoted herself to writing a book, called *20 hrs. 40 min.*, about her famous flight on the *Friendship.* The early days of flying offered many opportunities to make or break new records. Amelia was anxious to make "firsts," to prove the ability of women pilots and to promote their role in aviation.

In 1928 she became the first woman to make a solo round-trip flight across the United States.

Amelia competed in the first Women's Air Derby in 1929. In that same year she helped form a women pilots group called the "Ninety Nines," after the number of its charter members. Amelia became the group's first president.

In 1930 she set three women's world speed records.

Amelia (fourth from right) is seen with fellow contestants in the first Women's Air Derby in 1929. Jokingly called "The Powder Puff Derby" by some male reporters, the Derby brought together famous women aviators who proved that women pilots were capable of long flights. Louise Thadden (fifth from right) came in first, Gladys O'Donnell (third from left) came in second, and Amelia was third.

"The effect of having other interests beyond those exclusively domestic works well. The more one does and sees and feels, the more one is able to do...."

In February, 1931 Amelia married George Putnam, who'd become her manager, publicist, and promoter. George encouraged Amelia to set new records for women pilots. Following her flights, he arranged for Amelia to write books and articles about her experiences, and to go on lecture tours.

As her fame spread, Amelia was better able to earn the money she needed for her many expenses. Not only did she support herself and send money to help her mother, she purchased newer and better-equipped planes that required great upkeep.

Two months after her marriage, she set an altitude record in an autogiro. A predecessor to the helicopter, the autogiro had a single propeller and could take off and land without a runway. A month later she flew it solo across the continent and back—another first.

LEFT: In spite of their extremely busy schedules, George and Amelia found time to relax at their Rye, New York, home.

RIGHT: This glamorous picture was taken shortly before their marriage.

Ever since her flight on the *Friendship*, Amelia had felt challenged to make her *own* solo flight across the Atlantic. This time she would not be just a passenger!

By May 20, 1932, she was ready.

Flying in her red Lockheed Vega, she set out at dusk from Harbor Grace, Newfoundland. Thirteen and a half hours later, she arrived somewhat off course in a pasture in Londonderry, Ireland. She was the first woman pilot to successfully make the Atlantic crossing.

I taxied to the upper end of a sloping pasture

and turned my plane into the shelter of some trees....

Of course, I came down in a pasture and I had to circle many other

pastures to find the best one. The horses, sheep, and cows

in Londonderry were not used to airplanes, and so, as I flew low,

they jumped up and down and displayed certain disquiet."

LEFT: After landing in the Gallaghers' pasture (seen on pages 32–33), Amelia stopped at their farmhouse to wash her face and drink some tea. The next day, once the news of her arrival had spread, she read some of the congratulatory telegrams.

RIGHT: Crowds came out to cheer Amelia with a New York ticker-tape parade.

During the Atlantic crossing, the Vega's engines had used up 350 gallons of gasoline. Amelia drank one can of tomato juice, which she sipped through a straw.

Amelia's record flight was an exciting one. She discovered that her altimeter was faulty, so she was unable to record the plane's height above the sea. She encountered a violent storm and, trying to climb out of it, developed ice on her wings.

She said later, "I descended to hunt for warmer air to melt the ice. Down I went until I could see the whitecaps through the fog. It was unpleasant there, because sudden heavy fog and a dip would land me in the ocean. So I climbed until the ice began to form again. Then down again to the fog above the waves." Relying on her wits, she kept the plane above the water and below the altitude where ice formed.

Amelia's courage and persistence were matched by her spirit of adventure. Her pioneering sky voyage was acclaimed not only in the United States, but in many parts of the world.

Amelia received the National Geographic Society's Special Gold Medal from President Hoover. The ceremony was broadcast on radio so that the entire country could listen. (No TV in those days!)

Amelia received many awards that same year. Among them were the first Distinguished Flying Cross given to a woman by the United States Congress, and the Cross of the Legion of Honor from France.

At the White House, Amelia holds the National Geographic Society's Special Gold Medal, presented to her by President Hoover in 1932. In the group from left to right are: Dr. Gilbert Grosvenor, President of the Society; President Hoover; Amelia Earhart; and Mrs. Hoover. In the back row are: George Putnam and Dr. John Oliver La Gorce, of the Society. TOP RIGHT: The medal is given to honor those who demonstrate exceptional geographic achievement. It had been bestowed on only 12 men since 1906. Amelia was the first woman to receive it.

President Hoover said: *"She has shown a splendid courage and skill....*
She has often before demonstrated her ability to accomplish the most difficult tasks
that she set herself to do. She has been modest and good humored.
All these things combine to place her in spirit with the great pioneering women
to whom every generation of Americans has looked up....
The nation is proud that an American woman
should be the first woman in history to fly an airplane alone
across the Atlantic Ocean."

In 1933, the Rumanian Ambassador (center) presented
Col. Charles A. Lindbergh and Amelia Earhart
with medals from his government.

BELOW: Amelia practiced inflating an emergency raft in the event of a forced landing at sea.

RIGHT AND FOLLOWING PAGE: Ten thousand admirers greeted the smiling Amelia when she arrived in Oakland.

After her solo Atlantic flight, Amelia kept looking for new experiences. She loved to take to the skies, and wanted to set new records. She liked the challenge and the thrill of achieving, and she liked the fun of it.

In 1935 she began preparations for the flight that would eventually make her the first woman to fly solo across the Pacific Ocean from Hawaii to Oakland, California. Her food for the trip consisted of tomato juice, one hard-boiled egg, and a cup of delicious hot chocolate.

The night I found over the Pacific was a night of stars.

They seemed to rise from the sea and hang outside

my cockpit window,

near enough to touch, until hours later

they slipped away into the dawn."

With the help of her husband, who made all the arrangements, and at the request of the Mexican government, Amelia decided to make a "goodwill" flight from Burbank, California, to Mexico. She strayed off course and landed in a village near Mexico City, startling the local inhabitants. Her plane was quickly surrounded by cowboys, villagers, cattle, goats, and chickens.

Flying on to Mexico City, Amelia was greeted by the President of Mexico. Lively festivals and colorful celebrations were the highlights of her visit.

ABOVE: George, who had flown ahead, was waiting for Amelia when she arrived in Mexico.

RIGHT: Amelia's official welcome in Mexico City included a gift of a traditional Mexican cowboy outfit in blue and silver and a colorful sombrero.

Her return trip was another record—a nonstop flight from Mexico City to Newark, New Jersey. She left Mexico after an early morning breakfast and arrived in New York at 10:30 p.m., in time for a late dinner.

Amelia attracted people wherever she went with her warm and friendly personality. She was an articulate public speaker who made hundreds of lecture tours around the country. She often expressed concern about the education of women: Why shouldn't they have the same experiences and career choices as men?

In particular, she deplored the lack of opportunities for women in aviation, and the unfairness of unequal pay for men and women who did similar work.

LEFT: Waiting for Amelia in New Jersey after she made her historic nonstop flight across the Gulf of Mexico, an excited crowd of over ten thousand people swarmed past the police escort, anxious to catch a glimpse of the daring pilot, or to touch her.

BELOW: Amelia and Eleanor Roosevelt shared a concern for the status of women. They were good friends and Amelia was often a guest at the White House during her visits to Washington.

The President of Indiana's Purdue University, Edwin C. Elliot, was so impressed when he heard Amelia speak that he invited her to come to Purdue for part of the year as a career counselor for nearly a thousand women students.

Amelia accepted, and at age 38 she joined the faculty. Purdue had an aeronautics department and its own airfield. To Amelia's delight the university encouraged women to study mechanics and engineering.

At Purdue, Amelia's dream—to become the first woman to fly around the world—came closer to a reality. She felt she had "just one more long flight in my system."

Perched on top of her plane, Amelia is joined by a group of female students at Purdue University. As a counselor, she helped them with career choices.

There was my belief that now and then women

should do for themselves what men have already done—

and occasionally what men have not done—

thereby establishing themselves as persons, and perhaps

encouraging other women

toward greater independence of

thought and action."

Amelia checked out the Electra with mechanics as part of the many preparations for her flight.

A jubilant Amelia posed with her twin-engine "flying laboratory."

Under the management of the Purdue Research Foundation, an all-metal, twin-engine Lockheed Electra 10E with the most modern equipment was built especially for her use.

Amelia was thrilled with her shiny new Electra. The plane was built to meet the challenges of the arduous journey she was planning, with enough horsepower in the engines to accommodate the weight of additional fuel tanks.

Men had flown around the world, but Amelia's plan was to take the longest route, one never tried before, along the Equator. After the flight, she planned to use the plane as a "flying laboratory" to add to aviation research.

The preparations for the trip included many hours of careful planning, trial flights to test equipment, and studying maps and charts to determine the exact route.

*L*iving with these maps and charts

was absorbing and instructive. My knowledge of geography—

at least theoretically—increased from week to week.

To sit in the sunshine…in my California home, tracking monsoons

to their lairs and appraising rainfalls in India and

take-off conditions at African airports,

was an adventure in itself."

ABOVE: Paul Mantz, a veteran pilot and old friend, advised Amelia on flight plans for the trip.

RIGHT: Capt. Harry Manning studies an instrument for providing celestial bearings. He was to have been the navigator on the original around-the-world flight. Because of scheduling conflicts, he reluctantly gave his job over to Fred Noonan.

Fred Noonan, a former navigator for Pan American, had made a dozen trips across the Pacific. Amelia described him as "tops among aerial navigators."

ON MARCH 17, 1937, starting from Oakland, California, on a westerly course, she arrived at her first stop, Honolulu, Hawaii. However, on takeoff from Honolulu there was a disastrous mishap, a crash which required extensive repairs. When the plane was ready again, Amelia decided to reverse her route because of seasonal changes in weather conditions. On May 21, 1937, she began for a second time the first leg of the around-the-world flight. This time she left California going east, to Miami, Florida, making several stops and testing out the plane. With her was her friend, an experienced navigator, Fred Noonan.

At the Florida airport, final mechanical checks were made, and on June 1, the sleek silver plane took off into the Miami sunrise. The equatorial flight around the world took them to Caripito, Venezuela, Amelia's first glimpse of South America, and her first sight of a jungle. Then, dipping below the Equator, they stopped in Fortaleza, Brazil.

The Electra's cockpit, with a pilot and copilot's seat, measured four feet eight inches in height, and four feet six inches in length and width. Its control board contained about fifty dials and gauges.

Honolulu

140°E   160°E   180°   160°W   140°W

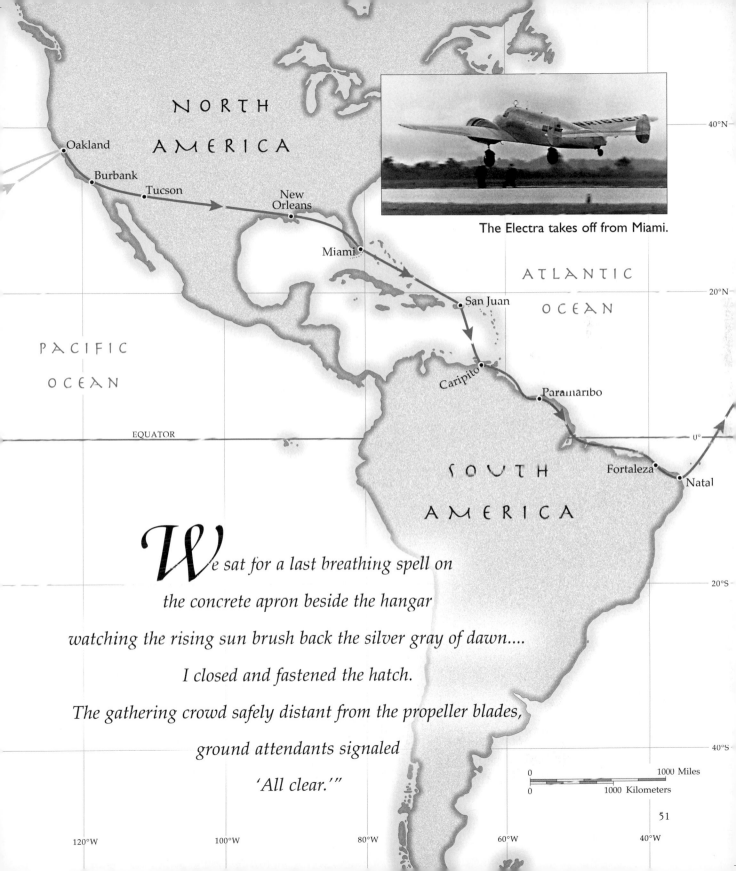

NORTH AMERICA

Oakland

Burbank

Tucson

New Orleans

Miami

PACIFIC OCEAN

ATLANTIC OCEAN

40°N

20°N

San Juan

Caripito

Paramaribo

EQUATOR

SOUTH AMERICA

Fortaleza
Natal

0°

20°S

The Electra takes off from Miami.

*W*e sat for a last breathing spell on

the concrete apron beside the hangar

watching the rising sun brush back the silver gray of dawn....

I closed and fastened the hatch.

The gathering crowd safely distant from the propeller blades,

ground attendants signaled

'All clear.'"

40°S

0   1000 Miles

0   1000 Kilometers

51

120°W   100°W   80°W   60°W   40°W

EUROPE

AFRICA

ARABIA

RED SEA

ARABIAN
SEA

A

Karachi

St. Louis
Dakar

Gao

N'Djamena

El Fasher

Khartoum

Massawa

Assab

INDIAN OCEAN

EQUATOR

After refueling at
Natal, Brazil, Amelia
and Fred flew northeast,
crossing the Equator for
the second time. Their
route took them over
the Atlantic and on
to the vast, mysterious
continent of Africa. Here
they made several stops for
refueling and equipment
checks. Thinking back to her
childhood in Atchison, Kansas,
Amelia said, "the dreams of long
ago had come true." She was visiting
the places that had been part of her flights
of fancy as a young child playing in the
carriage in her grandparents' barn.

The Electra received a good cleaning
at this stop in Africa.

0   1000 Miles
0   1000 Kilometers

20°W   0°   20°E   40°E   60°E

Beyond Africa lay the Red Sea, Arabia, and finally Karachi, in what is now Pakistan. In Karachi, while mechanics made repairs and an oil change, Amelia found time for some sightseeing. Intrigued by a bushy-bearded man in a high turban who offered rides on his camel, Amelia took the challenge in spite of Fred's teasing, "Better wear a parachute."

Whatever his disposition, my hired steed knelt down and I climbed into the saddle swung between his two humps. It was a startling take-off as we rose....As his hind legs unfold you are threatened with a nose-dive forward. Then with a lurch...the animal's center section hoists into the air."

With several others, Amelia went "cameling." She visited a nearby oasis, passing many other "ships of the desert" on the way. The Karachi airport was the largest she had seen, and an important stop for those flying from Europe to India and the Far East.

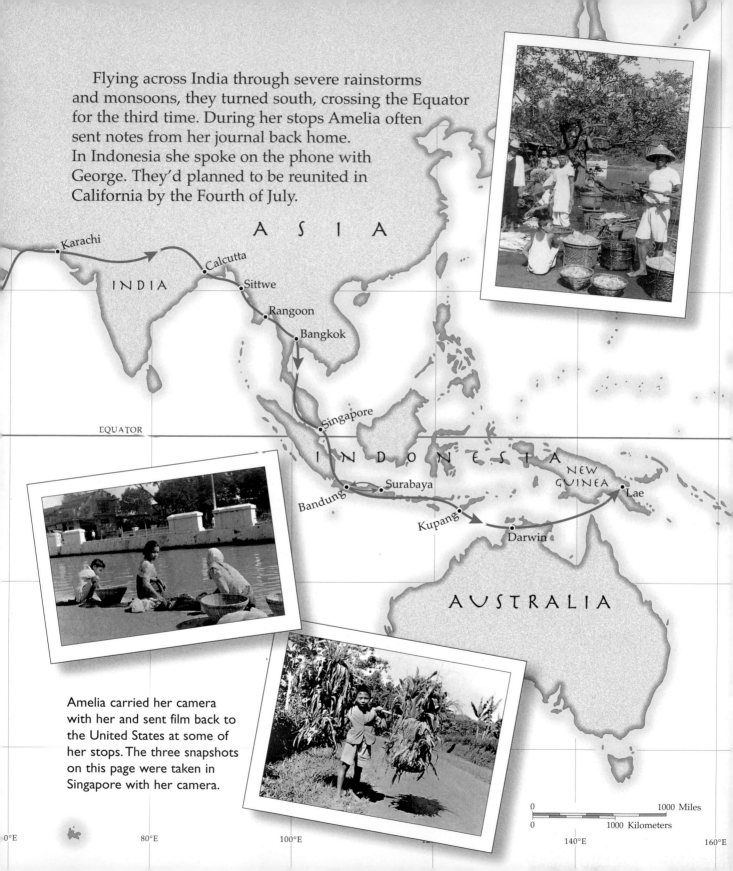

Flying across India through severe rainstorms and monsoons, they turned south, crossing the Equator for the third time. During her stops Amelia often sent notes from her journal back home. In Indonesia she spoke on the phone with George. They'd planned to be reunited in California by the Fourth of July.

ASIA

Karachi

Calcutta

INDIA

Sittwe

Rangoon

Bangkok

EQUATOR

Singapore

INDONESIA

NEW GUINEA

Lae

Bandung

Surabaya

Kupang

Darwin

AUSTRALIA

Amelia carried her camera with her and sent film back to the United States at some of her stops. The three snapshots on this page were taken in Singapore with her camera.

0   1000 Miles
0   1000 Kilometers

0°E   80°E   100°E   140°E   160°E

Fuel was siphoned from drums marked for Amelia Earhart at this stop in Indonesia.

On the 29th of June, Amelia and Fred arrived in Lae, New Guinea. They had been traveling almost six weeks and had covered the remarkable distance of 22,000 miles. But the most dangerous part of the trip lay ahead. They were to fly 2,556 miles over the Pacific Ocean to Howland Island, an island so tiny it would be difficult to locate.

EQUATOR ——————— 0°

PACIFIC ——————— 20°S

OCEAN

A smiling Amelia climbed out of her plane on arrival at Lae, New Guinea, her last stop before taking off for Howland Island.

——————— 40°S

120°W   100°W

55

On July 2, the Electra left New Guinea, heading toward Howland Island. Offshore, seamen aboard the U.S. Coast Guard cutter *Itasca* were waiting to guide the plane in for landing.

The *Itasca* received several radio messages from Amelia requesting a bearing. The crew replied each time, but Amelia did not acknowledge having heard them. Finally, more than five hours after her first message, she reported receiving their signals.

The cutter was unable to give her a bearing because her transmission was too brief.

The men aboard scanned the skies, anxious for a sighting.

Amelia's last message came less than an hour later. Attempting to find a radio frequency where they could make contact she said, "Listening on 6210 kilocycles. We are running north and south."

The *Itasca* crew tried to reach her on every possible radio frequency.

They received no further word.

There was only silence.

A massive sea and air search followed, but no trace has ever been found of the plane or its crew.

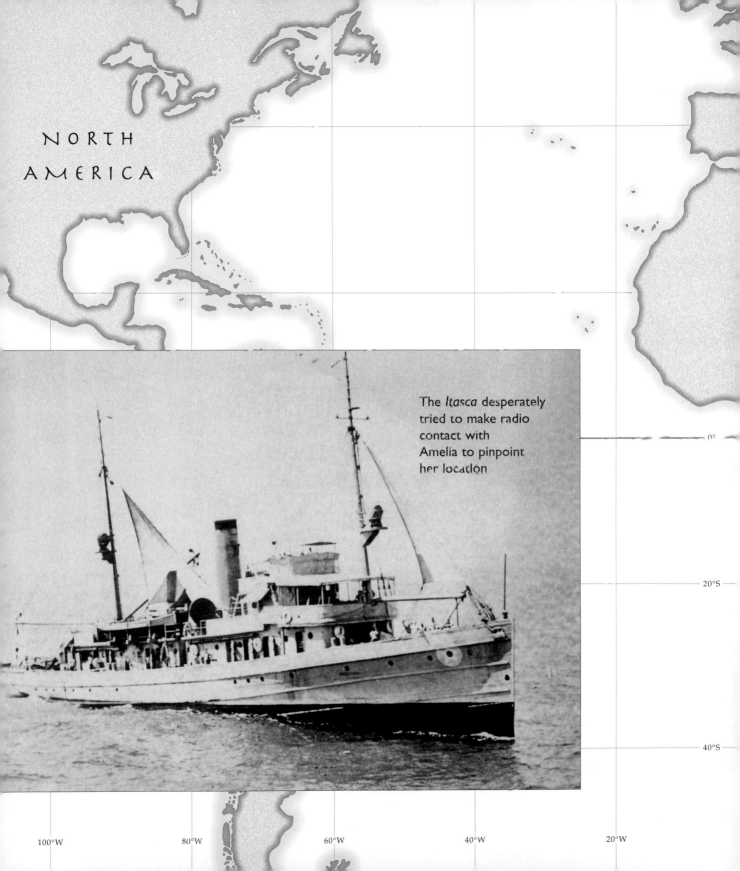

NORTH AMERICA

The *Itasca* desperately tried to make radio contact with Amelia to pinpoint her location

0°

20°S

40°S

100°W   80°W   60°W   40°W   20°W

*P*lease know I am quite aware of the hazards.
I want to do it because I want to do it.
Women must try to do things as men have tried.
When they fail, failure must be but
a challenge to others."

AFTERWORD

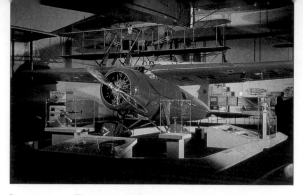

PREVIOUS PAGES: The Lockheed Electra takes off.
ABOVE: The red Lockheed Vega flown by Amelia in 1932 is hanging today in the Smithsonian Institution's Air and Space Museum, in Washington, D.C.

When someone vanishes without a trace, it becomes a mystery clamoring to be solved. This is the stuff that legends are made of. Amelia's last frantic words were sketchy and uninformative. Without definite proof of what happened, some people question whether she really disappeared. They look for clues, for answers to the inconclusive end of the world-famous pilot.

The speculation covers a wide range of theories. Some thought that Amelia was on a spy mission for the United States. Others suggested that she landed or crashed near one of the Pacific Islands and was picked up by the Japanese who patrolled that area. Could she have been imprisoned or executed by them? There was one bizarre speculation that she was rescued by the United States after World War II, sent home disguised as someone else, and given a new identity.

These theories were followed up by investigations, but were never proven to be true. In some cases they may have been prompted by people who, feeding on sensationalist rumors, wanted to gain fame for themselves. Both President Franklin Roosevelt and his wife, Eleanor, denied that Amelia was on a spy mission. Japanese records showed no evidence that she was found by one of their ships. All reputable investigations reported that there is no convincing evidence to substantiate any of these assumptions.

The attempt to explain her disappearance brought with it a series of "What ifs?" What if she and Noonan had been more experienced with Morse code? What if they had taken the extra-long antenna it was believed they left behind in Miami? What if they were not so exhausted by the time they reached Lae?

Both Amelia and Fred lacked a good working knowledge of Morse code. They had learned to fly without it. Instead they were relying on radio equipment that was exclusively based on voice contact. Being better at Morse code might have helped them to make contact with the *Itasca*. The 250-foot trailing antenna which was removed or shortened before the Electra left Miami might have made the difference in their ability to communicate and make themselves heard. Fatigue was certainly their enemy. Amelia and Fred had been traveling for more than thirty days, adjusting to different climates, often getting little sleep. This may have made it more difficult to concentrate and to use good judgment.

At best, this speculation is intriguing to read about. However, proof is something we may never entirely have. Unless someday her plane is found at the bottom of the ocean, closure may never take place.

For now, the only realistic conclusion is that her plane ran out of fuel and was lost at sea.

The real "afterword" to Amelia's story lies in a prophecy she made as she wrote about her thoughts on future air travel. She looked back more than a hundred years to the first women aeronauts, pioneers who flew in hot air balloons, and asked herself what changes in aeronautical activity would come in the next hundred years. She envisioned faster planes flying at higher altitudes, greater comfort for passengers, and the acceptance of flying as the best means of transportation for going anywhere in the world. She foresaw that "women will share in these endeavors, even more than in the past."

Amelia Earhart, sky pioneer, contributed to the fulfillment of this prophecy.

She paved the way for the thousands of women in aviation who followed her, from Air Force pilots, to captains on commercial planes, to women astronauts traveling in space.

CHRONOLOGY

July 27, 1897	Born in Atchison, Kansas, to Edwin and Amy Otis Earhart
1908	Saw her first airplane at the Iowa State Fair
1916	Entered the Ogontz School near Philadelphia, Pennsylvania
1918	Became a nurse's aide at Spadina Military Hospital in Toronto, Canada
1919	Enrolled as a premedical student at Columbia University in New York
1920	Visited her parents in Los Angeles, and took her first airplane ride
1921	Took her first flying lessons from Neta Snook
1922	Bought her first plane
	Set women's altitude record of 14,000 feet on October 22
1923	Received pilot's license on May 16
1926	Became a social worker at Denison House in Boston
1928	Became first woman to fly across the Atlantic as a passenger, June 17–18
	Was the first woman to make a round trip solo flight across the United States
1929	Took third place in the first Women's Air Derby
1930	Set women's speed record of 181 miles per hour
1931	Married George Putnam, February 7
	Set autogiro altitude record of 18,451 feet
1932	Became first woman to fly solo across the Atlantic, May 20–21
	Received the National Geographic Society's Special Gold Medal, June 21
	Set women's transcontinental speed record from Los Angeles, California, to Newark, New Jersey, August 24–25
1933	Broke her previous women's transcontinental speed record from Los Angeles, California, to Newark, New Jersey, July 7–8
1935	Became first person to fly solo from Honolulu, Hawaii, to Oakland, California, January 11–12
	Became first person to fly solo from Los Angeles, California, to Mexico City, April 19–20
	Became first person to fly solo from Mexico City to Newark, New Jersey, May 8
	Joined the faculty of Purdue University as a career consultant to women, September 1
1937	Attempted flight around the world

SELECTED READING

The quotes used in this book have been taken from Amelia Earhart's own writings, cited below, and from the September 1932 *National Geographic Magazine* coverage of the Special Gold Medal Award ceremony.

Earhart, Amelia. "Flying the Atlantic," *American Magazine*, August 1932.
_____. *The Fun of It*. New York: Brewer, Warren & Putnam, 1932.
_____. *Last Flight*. New York: Harcourt Brace and Company, 1937.
_____. *20 Hrs. 40 Min.: Our Flight on the* Friendship. New York: G.P. Putnam's Sons, 1928.
Lovell, Mary. *The Sound of Wings*. New York: St. Martin's Press, 1989.
Moolman, Valerie. *Women Aloft*. Alexandria, Virginia: Time-Life Books, 1981.
Morrissey, Muriel. *Courage Is the Price*. Wichita, Kansas: McCormick-Armstrong, 1963.
_____ and Osborne, Carol. *Amelia, My Courageous Sister*. Santa Clara, California: Osborne Publisher Inc., 1987.
Putnam, George Palmer. *Soaring Wings*. New York: Harcourt, Brace and Company, 1939.
Rich, Doris L. *Amelia Earhart*. Washington, D.C : Smithsonian Institution Press, 1989.

BOOKS WRITTEN ESPECIALLY FOR YOUNG READERS:

Lauber, Patricia. *Lost Star*. New York: Scholastic, Inc., 1988.
Shore, Nancy. *Amelia Earhart*. New York: Chelsea House Publishers, 1987.

ILLUSTRATION CREDITS

Cover, pp. 22 (lower), 26, 58–59, Corbis-Bettmann; pp. 2–3, 18, 38–39, 44–45, 46–47 (both), 51, 52–53 (both), 54–55 (all), Purdue University; pp. 5, 19, 28–29, The Ninety-Nines, Inc., International Organization of Women's Pilots; pp. 6–7, 32–33, 37 (lower), 40, 48 (right), back dust jacket, AP/Wide World Photos; pp. 8, 9 (lower), 10–11 (both), 12, 16, 30, 35, 48 (left), The Schlesinger Library, Radcliffe College; pp. 9 (upper), 23, 34, 60, National Air and Space Museum, Smithsonian Institution; pp. 12–13, 14–15, State Historical Society of Iowa, Des Moines; p. 17 (both), American Red Cross; p. 20–21, Courtesy of Sally Putnam Chapman; pp. 22 (upper), 24–25, 36, UPI/Corbis-Bettmann; pp. 26–27, The Pond Bureau; pp. 27, 31, Library of Congress; p. 37 (upper), National Geographic Society Photographers; pp. 38, 41 (right), George Palmer Putnam; pp. 41 (left), 49, Seaver Center for Western History Research, Los Angeles County Museum of Natural History; pp. 42–43, 57, National Archives; p. 43, Underwood and Underwood; p. 50, Albert L. Bresnick; Front and back dust jacket (background), Larry Lee/West Light.

INDEX

Photographs are indicated by **boldface**. If photographs are included within a page span, the entire span is boldface. When another person appears in a photograph with Amelia Earhart, the picture reference is under that person's entry.

CORINNE SZABO has an MFA in painting from
American University in Washington, D.C. A former teacher,
she is a graphic designer and a photo researcher who has
worked on exhibits, CD-ROMs, television documentaries,
and publications. While gathering pictures of Amelia
Earhart, Corinne Szabo became fascinated by their diversity.
She read Earhart's own books about her flights,
then turned to other sources to deepen her knowledge.
The author says, "When I learned about Amelia Earhart's
outlook on how to live her life—to do the things
one likes best, to speak up for what one believes in,
to see life as a great adventure, to be 'true to oneself'—
I wanted to tell young people her story."
Corinne Szabo and her husband, Dan,
live in Rockville, Maryland.

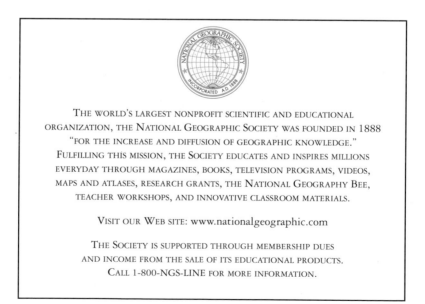

THE WORLD'S LARGEST NONPROFIT SCIENTIFIC AND EDUCATIONAL
ORGANIZATION, THE NATIONAL GEOGRAPHIC SOCIETY WAS FOUNDED IN 1888
"FOR THE INCREASE AND DIFFUSION OF GEOGRAPHIC KNOWLEDGE."
FULFILLING THIS MISSION, THE SOCIETY EDUCATES AND INSPIRES MILLIONS
EVERYDAY THROUGH MAGAZINES, BOOKS, TELEVISION PROGRAMS, VIDEOS,
MAPS AND ATLASES, RESEARCH GRANTS, THE NATIONAL GEOGRAPHY BEE,
TEACHER WORKSHOPS, AND INNOVATIVE CLASSROOM MATERIALS.

VISIT OUR WEB SITE: www.nationalgeographic.com

THE SOCIETY IS SUPPORTED THROUGH MEMBERSHIP DUES
AND INCOME FROM THE SALE OF ITS EDUCATIONAL PRODUCTS.
CALL 1-800-NGS-LINE FOR MORE INFORMATION.